Sandberry Press

CALLING CARDS: NEW POETRY FROM CARIBBEAN/CANADIAN WOMEN

The six women whose poems appear in this book are new voices. Only one, Mary Lou Soutar-Hynes, has previously published a collection of her own. The poetry of Celia Ferrier and the late Keisha Silvera appears here for the first time. Nan Peacocke, Janet Somerville and Jennifer Walcott have published poems in journals and anthologies in Canada and abroad. Four of these poets were born in other countries and chose to make Canada their home, three being born in the Caribbean. The youngest, a powerful talent, died early. Their signatures on these poetic calling cards are distinctive.

Caribbean Poetry Series

1. *Loggerhead*
Gloria Escoffery

2. *A Tale from the Rainforest*
Edward Baugh

3. *Journey Poem*
Pamela Mordecai

4. *Strategies*
Dennis Scott

5. *Rain Carvers*
Judy Hamilton

6. *Flame Tree Time*
Elaine Savory

7. *Fellow Traveller*
Jane King

8. *It Was the Singing*
Edward Baugh

9. *The True Blue of Islands*
Pamela Mordecai

Anthology Series

1. *Calling Cards*
Celia Ferrier, Nan Peacocke, Keisha Silvera, Janet Somerville, Mary Lou Soutar-Hynes, Jennifer Walcott

CALLING CARDS
New Poetry from
Caribbean/Canadian Women

Celia Ferrier
Nan Peacocke
Keisha Silvera
Janet Somerville
Mary Lou Soutar-Hynes
Jennifer Walcott

Sandberry Press
Toronto   Kingston

Copyright © Pamela Mordecai 2005

All rights reserved. No part of this publication may be reproduced, stored in a retrieval system or transmitted in any form or by any means without the prior written permission of the publisher.

A catalogue in publication record of this book is available from Library and Archives Canada

Anthology series: No. 1
Series editor: Pamela Mordecai

ISBN: 1-894528-02-6

Published by Sandberry Press, 446 Bartlett Avenue, Toronto, Ontario, M6H 3G7, Canada, and 21 Holborn Road, Kingston 10, Jamaica, W. I.
e-mail: sandberry@sympatico.ca

Set in Palatino and made in Toronto by Sinai
Cover photograph: Martin Mordecai
Cover design: Robert Harris
Publishing consultant: Shivaun Hearne

Printed and bound in Canada

TABLE OF CONTENTS

1. Time Past

CELIA FERRIER
Pointe aux Pins stories   11

NAN PEACOCKE
Memory   16
You No Send, Me No Come   17
River   18
The Inheritance   19

KEISHA SILVERA
Mama 21
I am sitting in a chair   23
Thick and viscous with ripe fertility 24
This air it worries me   25

JANET SOMERVILLE
Grandpa's Matchbook   26
Epiphany   27
I Try to Imagine My Father   28
Off Lakeshore Drive   29
June 7, 1994   32

MARY LOU SOUTAR-HYNES
at the whim/of fault lines   34
to a creole ancestor   35
survivor's song   36
by invitation   37
maybe   38

JENNIFER WALCOTT
Name Sake 39
Sepia Print 40
Still Life 41
Orchid Lady 42
A Search for Roots – Distaff Side 43
Sgraffito 44
Fairy Tale 45

2. Time Present

CELIA FERRIER
cliché & cruelty 48
Petersham Common 50
remember the tree 52
Virginia girl 53
Toronto 2 a.m. 55

NAN PEACOCKE
Headwound 57
Parallax 59
Winnipeg via Rail 60
Pain-ting 61

KEISHA SILVERA
what lives in the clouds 62
nine o'clock appointment 63
& then there's the other side of the street 66
Lipstick 67
American Gothic 68
oranges 69

JANET SOMERVILLE
Calling Card   70
Italian Touring Tips   71
On These Shores   72
Rowing the Inner Harbour at 6 a.m.   73
Chez Pierre   74
At the Pietà   75

MARY LOU SOUTAR-HYNES
after/shocks   77
beyond the edge   78
tufetto sands   79
harbour front lounge:/casino halifax   81
transit sighting   83

JENNIFER WALCOTT
San Woman   84
Bathurst and Queen   85
Scars   86
Cerasee   87
Cartoon   88
Mapping   89
Split Infinitive   90

CONTRIBUTORS   92

EDITOR'S NOTE   94

ABOUT SANDBERRY PRESS   96

1. Time Past

CELIA FERRIER

Pointe aux Pins Stories

1
under pine darkness
in brown needle beds
on stiff plastic basket webs
folding chairs open
their long limbs released
from lunch dishes done
before dinner dishes down
their legs decorated
veins popped like tattoos
from copper brushed clavicles
breast pendulums hung
elbows crooked into cradles
calves made into cages
we clung for balance
to mothery movements
slackened silk softness
a syncopated music
for each child bellied
our infant visions
of silver-scaled fingers
tender tonic palms
whispered rests wove
gracious gossip we
witnessed their noses and toes curl
lines light up their cheeks
raised theatre curtains
their eyelids and lips
acting a drama
for spellbound spectators
of their matinee

2
i was a wayward child no use denying that
tugged the table cloth 'til winewatercandlewax
landed in their laps
i dropped grandma's china dishes
which skittered like mice across the floor
i slammed the door
glass crystal diamonds showered the gravel drive
i disturbed the hive
stepped over caution lines pulled at errant threads
picked at every scab unraveled every stitch
questioned every rule examined every pit
handled every knife
and i told Anton he should not hit his wife

3
there was a blue chair
in the corner where i dreamed
and i would have turned out the light
sucked ink black
into blotting paper triangles
if i had known the order then

in that same corner i played
the piano hours through time
was corrected and wept
was allowed to trail
myself after the hot flue
of a turquoise vacuum cleaner
spine shiver to dissolve care
forget behind the chair
with the picture of an absence
in my hand

then there were patches
in the music practiced
brown and green and orange
and there were vinyl records
blue and red and gold
but i couldn't hear the sea
i was told there would be
i listened i heard notes
saw cascades of quavers
but not waves not even
imaginary ones

4
O how his invitation elevated with its choosing and how
the nine-year-old Iphegenia was taken down the river
to a very undistinguished spot a low reedy bank where
the shit of the town shifted down and settled into
stinking sludge not solid river mud

O how her father made of her an order of war
how his words were weapons he said his issue
were like fishes hatched from eggs held five minnows
a moment then poured them out over the side
in the belly of the boat how he gutted the fertile fish flung
its prophetic entrails out for birds

5
freighters sound
through the fog
float their call
into our dreams
our haunts
we five
float lies
we stay alive

6
i didn't know then and knew too late
when the ten storey ship
passed like a colossal python
in the slow depth of the channel
sand banked as i was
i would narrowly
just narrowly escape
and come as near to hell
as it is possible to come
the black iron ton that skinned
the water raw and i
just partially submerged
as near to death
as anyone can
in this relative world get
as close as two arms length

7
amid tropical gardenias so out of place
on a northern May morning
when outdoors there is no green bulb
able to break the frost
when inside the only other bulb will
not bloom until autumn
the bride buries her weeds
in silken sleeves
car tires scream but do not
substitute a doe and spirit her
to Iphegenia's island

8
a window a blue chair and a son
i know i have one
though sometimes i know i don't

and now that wished for one
i saw out the window
from behind the curtains
and the tree branches
and along the asphalt street
the s curve path of snakes
flattened by cars into hot tar
iron black smell of ship oil slicks
which separate tree
from tree and ditch from
ditch still only exist like that
in memory
he is and was and will be
he is material but not present
he is completely of another order
now being flesh

NAN PEACOCKE

Memory
ojo's treatise on DNA

Ancestor stands up mudgreen and great in the knee-deep delta. Cast in a purple dawn, she wades the Bocas, infant Antillian riding her back. A runner now, she lives on shells and pods, forager of pieces. To the child she feeds herself. At night she learns how the moon spells. Taino priest now, she picks a bow from the forest. On the beach glints a shattered stone. A seeker now, she arcs her arm compass from river to sky fish, draws her arrow and releases it. Her strong arrow circles the earth and returns, wounding the child on her back.

You No Send, Me No Come
In the Cockpit Country of Jamaica many lose their way

I ask Limestone,
What goes on in there?
Is the mind an undiscovered cave?
Labyrinth mysterious
formed drip by drip
inna millennia?
She lets us recall her maps of earth,
of stars,
of DNA even
but keeps to herself the place where her own simple
sketches
lie hidden.
She lets us not know her.
Tricky.

River

Africa looks back at us now. And I saw the Amerindian nations look back. And all the tribes, the Scots, the Portuguese and Dutch, Asia's all. I saw it happen up the Orinoco with Wilson the oarsman and my brother, Trevor. The boat climbed up the river bearing us. Farsighted Wilson in the stern dipped the oar and wrote it out and dipped it in again. My brother held an oar at the prow. Without Wilson in his line of vision, he listened, making their paddle one.

  We passed through the brown passage of the river. The river passed through us. Behind us the river became the truncated bend of where we had been. Ahead of us the curve we would describe awaited. Curving into that bend in the river, our vessel moved to starboard and the forest stood before me – before anyone.

  I was looking at the pose of trees, but seeing too my brother. His limbs dancing from the shoulders, repeating the trees. The forest motioned through us, back down the river from where we had come. My brother, who had been paddling in Wilson's rhythm, stopped. He looked back at me anchored to the anchor of now. Suspended in the passage of the river, in the passage of no time, just, just, just.

  Then I too looked back, and then Wilson, back, back. World without end.

The Inheritance
For Nora

Early that morning
pain laid you back into the geography
and all our long journey
of love and conflict
the incredulous household
the drops of water I rubbed across your lips
were nothing
against that
one
quick
blow

Finally
I shut away
the mild surprise
still
in your eye

That night
keeping watch from this side
I followed your windy dessert crossing
till these poor instruments
could no longer sight
your sheet white hair
sailing to glory

Into a hole in the hillside
we let the satchel slip

I shuddered at the ghastly
clinking
unloosed
buckles

My brother
leaning inward
said
Remember, that's not her there

Not you
You're not here now
That you lived is certain
under a mackerel sky
with your flowers
your insistence
that you counted
and were counted

and parted
this universal loneliness
counts me
strangely
among the believers.

KEISHA SILVERA
Mama

Mama
      through this narrow hall
      walls squeezing limbs
          I can't get to you
      through this squeamish
      back & forth
          my senses are tired
I could believe that you are floating
with the clouds above my head
I could believe that it is you
replacing my fear with tears
          Where are you?

You held my baby body
after the doctor smacked my
bottom
now it is forever you who does the
smacking
It confuses me past & future
  Time
My present is your past from
now on
  Where are you?

This is not what I want
This is life
Death
This is here to be figured out
I know I will be so much

stronger sturdier more like
you were and that fucks me
up that you are past tense.

How impotent the physical is
How communication had been
taken for granted

In my blood you are my blood
& you were my beginning

I am sitting in a chair

I am sitting in a chair that is filled with you.
You sit in it every evening & watch the nightly news.
I am sitting in this chair waiting for you.
Seeing if I can trace that part of you that is real
or maybe I can remember something you've said
absurd or not
        i miss you
        i miss you
        i miss you

Thick and viscous with ripe fertility

Thick and viscous with ripe fertility
of mould and maggots.
Roll in it. And swallow
swallow me down lumps & all
in the same place. Huddled together the air
mixed with individual breathing.
We breath it all in and for one long second
we can't tell who's who. Am I you
in this silhouette to be all dark and
inaccessible
inaccessible is terribly attractive. Beat
myself against your walls only to find I was
sitting somewhere else and you were in the
Great Wall of China pretending to be a
skeleton under Bedlam
Bedlam right now is half eaten peanut butter
lipstick blotted tissues
dirty knives
& sweet and lo

This air it worries me

  This air it worries me
it is that each quiver
of the wind
seems to want to push me off the
edge of this place
Vast blue with cracks for screams
I stand throwing you up in the air
over and over   pretending you could
be alive
and I think if I try really hard I can
reach my arm in
let it squirm like seaweed
strain for the volumes living in the space behind your tongue
the brutal curl of your talk
your smell ingrained   taunting my sentiment
and I'm waiting for a time when you no longer fill
in my distraction
I will wake up in cold relief   chilled
as a newborn baby
with her heart in her palm

JANET SOMERVILLE
Grandpa's Matchbook

Grandpa's matchbook cover
was always tucked
in the breast pocket
of a short-sleeved
cotton collared shirt

its faded cover
boasted hand-carved oak furniture
by a competitor in Paris, Ontario
its matches lit
twenty-eight king-sized
DuMaurier Extra Mild

its corner removed
wandering threads
of beef and parsley
as his tongue
sucked and clicked
against front teeth

its inside cover
a litany of directions
for a final ride
by way of Humphrey's funeral parlour
to plot number 2080
in Mount Pleasant cemetery

Epiphany

When she was twenty-one
my mother discovered her father

living in Kingston Penitentiary
imprisoned for fraud

a swindle greater than his
committed by her dead mother's relatives:

maiden aunts spun trickster tales
about a worthless husband

his memory buried
clods of dirt

suffocating their sister Helen
those eighteen years

I am given another truth forty years later
as I hold my dying aunt's swollen hand:

she insists my grandfather Dwight
was too kind for his own good

I Try to Imagine My Father

I try to imagine my father
as the boy he was in the photograph
where his head cocks to the left

and his fingers curve through the gills
balancing the dead weight
of the speckled trout

eyes glossy marbles
he's twelve or thirteen
as he poses beside his own father

who surely roused him
from his adolescent slumber before the sun
in the front room of the little cabin in Muskoka

with the wooden screened door
that creak slaps open and shut
open and shut on rusting hinges

Off Lakeshore Drive

In 1976
my great uncle Wes
plants himself
in a worn swivel chair
in the front room

>   taps out wet tobacco
>   from a Player's tin
>   with his missing
>   trigger finger

>   He licks the rolling paper
>   the tip of his tongue
>   a slug inching along
>   his chapped lower lip

>   twirls the stick
>   between nicotined fingers
>   familiar with rifles

This man I fear
with his regulation
brush cut gestures
with his stump
to the black and white tv
where another man
in hipwaders guts a pickerel

>   and I consider
>   the fates of
>   the smooth speckled
>   army green bait frogs

       in the aluminum tub
       beyond the back
       wooden screened door
       that creak slaps
       open and shut
       open and shut

I think of the warning stories
I've been told and retold
him passing out stone cold

by the big rock in the bush
where we meet to
pick wild blueberries

Missing for days
he'd stumble about
in a cheap whisky stupor
a hunter-knight errant
in search of quail deer or bear
reinventing himself
in familiar fictions

a good father
a good husband
a good soldier

       But really
       I know
       Wes was ready
       to snap

his mind coiled
around life's disappointments

neither doctor lawyer
nor Indian chief
and childless from
shame decades old

when Peg bound herself
in swathes of cotton rags

and choked the growing
child inside

another man's pride
and her guilt their curse

    Toby Tina or Rex
    short-haired musty hounds
    and hunting companions
    soften this memory

    surrogate children
    spoiled in summer
    by thick slices
    of vanilla ice cream
        curled at his slippered feet
            paws flicking
                they chase dream squirrels

June 7, 1994

In Bracebridge she slides you
out of your chilled drawer
and – unlike the other faceless fatality –
you are yourself

Head turned to the side
and covered behind in gauzy white cloth
to protect my eyes
from the shredded
horror underneath

I know it's you because
you're wearing the striped shirt
I gave you for your last birthday
(you were twenty-four then)

Your black blood
gelled and pooling
 by your mouth
surprises me

Afraid I'd touch you or
tamper with evidence
I'm invigilated by the cop
who dragged you
from the lake
early this morning

You are readied
for your final ride,
as Grandma used to say
matter-of-factly

She's here today
elegant with
her nails painted
as you'll remember
Revlon's Windsor Rose

Grandpa's here too
shuffling up the aisle
swearing, wishing
he could trade places
with you

They've coiffed you
but I can't keep myself
from messing up your
picture-perfect hair
or looking for
that patch of rough skin that
defies the undertaker's razor

They've propped your hands
across your chest
(I'm grateful that your fingernails aren't clean)

I've tried to be thoughtful
Even made you a tape
of your favorite tunes:
I hope you don't think
I'm being too sentimental
I don't want you to be without
Neil, or Cat, or Garth ever

MARY LOU SOUTAR-HYNES
at the whim/of fault-lines

              islands   ebb and flow
constant   in their small certainties
      captured
from the air   in one exposure
circumnavigated
easily

fold-mountain contradictions
      intersecting   layer-on-layer
as shells   from headstrong seas
surface on hillsides

              volcanoes sleep   breathe lush
      gardens   lava-fires   wait
rio-cobre valleys   carve deep   ragged-
        edged

island contours   in the
      blood —
where even the earth   moves

at the whim   of fault-lines

to a creole ancestor
from the series "to a creole ancestor"

        to a creole
             ancestor

                your traces
linger   in our naked
moments
speak colourless truths   when
the moon is
    new —

                       we   are your text
            your poignant
       enigmas
    re-weaving
tangled
       tales —

          while you lie silent
in shadows   of our un-knowing —
    shedding light

survivor's song
from the series "to a creole ancestor"

                survivor's song

           you
        carve   textured
     shadows   in
the face of stones —
deep petroglyphs   with billowing
    sails
          your molten rock   red-orange
              cooled to
                    black   rain-forests
                      misting

lava's smouldering skin   the restless paths
      of flow —   like hot wax
           bleeding

by invitation
from the series "to a creole ancestor"

        by invitation

                beyond the windward side
           of islands   where
      tides dance —
we step into your silence

            feel its velvet   buoyancy
               its dark salt   anointing
                  the tongue

                        — deep ocean's
                  intimate
            undulations   the teeth
     of reefs —   your
  wave pools   naked
 breaking
sweat

maybe
from the series "to a creole ancestor"

       maybe

      it is the sea
    that bears   memory's
      weight   riding nightly on
       the whale's
         back —
                   as blood-
              moons remember   pale
          clouds   autumn's early sigh   shiver
 of tide pools —
              maybe
 this is   ocean's siren pull —
sweetening rivers   spilling dreams   into the mouths of
    seas   formless recollections
      in the deep

                    drifts   quiet as light—
                   tongues   on
                      fire

JENNIFER WALCOTT
Name Sake

Over here, I turn and turn again, trying to find
the whisper of a skirt that will lead me to a name.
The mother of my mother's mother's mother.

I've heard that over there they sing lullabies,
whisper softly the names of the stolen away.

Perhaps the name I seek is in a song,
being sung right now, released into the air,
riding the Harmattan or the Warm Braw.

Sepia Print

Granny was always old
wore her mended stockings
rolled round her fat knees,
underpants hewn from bleached
sacks for chicken feed.

Granny was always old
white mustache and yellowed
hair, a round barrel belly
she bathed twice a week
sitting on a wooden chair.

Granny was always old
her drooping breasts beyond
the cure of bay rum on
the secret sores hidden
in her patched white sheets.

Granny was always old
threw away nothing

except her life.

Still Life

A memory, perhaps, propels this motion
or, maybe my mother's hands move restless
just to show they're still alive.

They are travelers, paper-thin
wrinkled skin and bone
they move unceasingly
an agitated back and forth
her purse, her lap
the chair, my back.

Orchid Lady

Twisted feet like orchid roots
curled round tradition,
tied her down to hearth and home
secured by parents' fears.
She fed the young ones Chopin
pound cake, sticky toffee,
drove them mad
in her little Morris Minor,
taught them to love
and care for gardens.

Transplanted, grafted, nourished
on food fads and homeopathy,
she thrived. Flowered late and long,
showered brothers' old and new wives
and their young
with her blossoming.

Then she withered – lost her scents,
lay pressed between
the bed sheets and her age.

Oh, lay her flat, the nurses said,
she's traveling today.
Wrap her in tissue shrouds, send her on her way.

A Search for Roots – Distaff Side

Quiet, eyes downcast,
their iron cores insist
we meet their few demands:
the hurricane marriage
bamboo sliver insult
sour orange life.
That we know of them was all they asked.

But all the other stories that we yearn for
are swept away, like cobwebs,
gone with the old women and
we're left gazing at a darkening sky.

Sgraffito

Look inna de pictcha good.
Yu' see say de fadda ha'
Him han' roun' de gal pickney dem?

Dat han' nevah use fe hug.

If yu' was to scrape off
de surface a de pictcha
yu' woulda see de knife
wha' him use fe stab de gal
dem in dem back.
How him cut dem heart
an' lef dem hungry,
fe fill dem belly
wid fadda love.

Dis ya pictcha
no show how dem tek dem
self-esteem fe stuff up
hole, nyam dirt, an' spit
blood, cut dem tongue on
sharp wud, an' cry.

Lawd, how dem cry.

Yu' haffi wuk fe see de
tears behin'
the laugh dem a laugh
in de lyin' photograph.

Fairy Tale

Three princesses under the spell of a wicked ogre
Who also happens to be the king their father.
But see, he's handsome, a real ladies' man,
Even though the lady queen has long flown the coop.
Seems she did not have a sweet tooth – was sick of his
sugar.
But those three girls, well, he lulled them into deep,
deep sleep.

The eldest fell right out of bed
into the arms of a stable man;
she's there to this day, making hay
come rain or come shine.
You might say she's lived a charmed life.

The middle one suffered
the fate of all middle children,
caught between high desperation
and low expectations,
she kept looking through a mirror
and got it all backwards.

The youngest? She took no
ball of twine with her on her travels,
covered her tracks so well
she circled back on herself many times
before she got wise, climbed a tree,
and taught the birds to speak.

2.Time Present

CELIA FERRIER
cliché & cruelty

she ran away from the circus
from the masks of clowns
their laughing leers
she wanted no cotton candy to dissolve
like hot pink sand
no sweet pink popcorn
to dye her tongue more red
than the tights of bare backed riders
wrinkled at the knee, the stalks
of withered elephants that stank
with fear and sweat and excrement
who shrank from electric prods
hooks that pierced the toughest skin
she would free them poor beasts
or help to kill their maulers

she ran from the roulette wheel
spun to stop on her dime
until the clerk behind the counter
moved his knee, she said so
she saw him claim it
his python hiss constrictor
gamble candy hushes all
don't spoil our illusions child
more afraid of truth
they choose the crook
they need the fiction
the glossy picture book that says
no more than 'c' for circus –

and commerce
and cowardice

clap for the dancing bear
stumble-drugged
clap for the monkeys masticating air
strung like heavy acrobats
clap for castrated pacing tigers
teased to frustrated roars
she means, clap when they don't perform
when their claws almost catch
when they veer from any practiced path
and run rings around
the animals we are
leave nothing but their urine behind
and when the freight departs
the rancid parking lot
she dreams of rail disasters

Petersham Common

Like follies in a garden miniature
from Richmond Hill manor houses glow
high Hampton Court spires a distant blur
white crown of Castle Windsor shows
while Twickenham Rugby hides Heathrow.

Below a green spotted with cows
canal boats punt the winding Thames
a dog's bark faint from a wood fades
fainter like the old who amble
by the Royal Star and Garter Home

for aging vets. One motors in
his wheelcart, bandaged over nose
and mouth: fifty years of pity,
awe and reverence. Against
the tidy terrace tourists pose.

We regard the scene museum-like
you can see that in the faces
of the girls who carry volumes: Pope,
Walpole, Woolf , or the mistress
of Marble Hill. We hold conversations

with the dead. Down along we drift
flanked by English oak, plane tree flakes
our leg oars dip in liquid earth beside
a floating shanty swamped by yachts
too big for this or any English lake

and all seems right in this world.
Fish jump, geese honk, children hop the steps

to downy swans that cruise for crumbs
under low and foamy clouds
where silver airplanes hover and hum

in a Reynolds sky. Pigeons chuckle
in the brush, wings whir against the leaves
swallows whimsically loop
or do they swoop for food? A golden hound
labours through the moss green stream.

Childrens' laughter blends to bird calls
all peeps and chirps; red shirts cross the lawn
they march like soldiers swinging arms
the dog floats its nose along the turf
barks as the harbour master trawls

for all is well. He watches
a low slung barge trail past,
a throb of metal music in its throat
as fashionable Fanny tilts
her torso through the hatch to catch

the breeze, restoringly chill. A snap
of pebbles under wheels, bike bell rings,
legs flash like wings and I am clipped,
common colonial, with a curse,
pop back through Bert's chalk drawing

where caramel and licorice cows
low and lumber artlessly, black crows in petticoats
and two-toned terns serve afternoon tea,
where peacocks squawk like monkeys,
and the jungle mocks this pastoral.

remember the tree

at fourteen in nineteen thirty-seven
my father hopped a freight to Temagami
with his seven-year-old brother

the only two stories he would tell me
were of stealing cans of food
which lead to stern words from the local copper

and of sleeping by a bend in the train tracks
one night waking up to the monster puffing
straight towards them screaming rails and steam

in his groggy blur he grabbed the scruff
of his brother's neck and stood frozen
not knowing which way to dive

was it right or left to safety
or would he leap into oncoming steel?

on the evening of the first of may a thunder crack
woke me from a dark sleep but there was no storm
no crashing plane or derailed train came through

my open window but the oppressed rain-laden tree
the fence-wrapped trunk next door dying for years
had fallen into the ravine finally free

the misty green night was more silent
and more alive than it had ever been

Virginia girl
Unlike the singing cicadas, the silent fireflies burn themselves. – Chinese proverb

after the evening chase
we opened the alley gate

passed through one by each
mother father me

why don't you tell her
he said

scent of boxwood
his smoking hand

april fire-flies
her flickering face

jar of blinking
beetles wanting release

how many remained
when she lay in a pink room

waiting for him
and her last breath

i will never tell her
she said

don't i imagine now
full grown and gate ajar

a dark brown head bobbed
just above that backyard fence

being mauled
by brutish paws

slack maw
and fragile girlhood fled

Toronto 2 a.m.
after Adam Zagajewski's "To Go to Lvov"

perhaps I can sit here
watch morning dawn in Paris
a low grey eye widening below La Tour Eiffel
trucks might be counted like sheep
their progress lurching like my fitful sleep

alone in Paris it would be the same
but only if Paris exists and the eye
which lights the horizon peers through
the tower standing blue aloof
beyond it bloodshot pink

at 7 a.m. I am waking up in Paris
sounds of traffic electric razors
showers hairdryers coffee makers
and the radio says minus two degrees and clear
in six minutes day has arrived if day exists

there is always too much of Paris
none can comprehend its arrondisments
is that La Défense in the distance
where smoke spills from the stacks
is that the dome of Sacré Coeur
is that the delivery truck for Micheline's
and is that Roland gone to the office so soon
is that Angelique, Claudine
me in the red coat on the corner
waiting for the light to change
turning like the other ghosts
who vanish as the webcam staggers
through bytes of ragged life?

the tower like lace now against a turquoise sky
the bright lid pushing morning up away
to sleep now that Paris is safely out of night
to see Montmartre there past the dark
where the steam billows in a wider arc

the sky is open now
the palest greenest eye
the last beignets et café
the last croissants du thé
7:25 and the temperature's holding

NAN PEACOCKE
Headwound

In this year's afternoon the painted trees watch summer debrief while I, ankle deep in the wake of an equinox, listen for the story of another fall. October's red tongues whisper to my parched ear but cannot give me word of my mother's other child – my twin, well past forty and likely drunk in a gutter somewhere south of here.

The summer of storms is behind us. In British Colombia we had firestorm. In Nova Scotia we had hurricane. Basements disgorged in south Ontario. Grenada flew. In Haiti, the statuesque dead buried themselves. Who wouldn't be glad of the end of it? In truth I miss the confusion. Now there's only waiting.

The lengthening geese flow sunward. We will stay put, like dogs chained to an approaching winter wave, stiff in midair. The season of spooks approaches wearing its orange silence. No passing goblins, no mild mannered ghosts bring me hopeful news of Morgan. Even the harvest moon, her famed largesse this year has no more to offer than a pockfaced pumpkin, a grimace of spaced out teeth, the vacant triangular eyes of a drunk.

I still hear our language in my head. In the place I was born it have walking dead, it have soukouyan, la diablesse, lagahoo. It have 'a man' different from 'a man in pieces'. It have 'house fall down' different from 'fallen house'. 'House fall down' could fix.

Together, the dog and I walk the sloping field to the river. Childplay sounds tinge our ears. Downstream, children from the Ontario village where

I now live, plunge a deep pool as it collects itself for the spillway. 'Watch this you guys'. On the embankment, the United Church looks on as one by one the kids leap off the concrete weir into another Ecclesiastical river – their pale bodies suspended Xs and Ys. My memory plunges a time in star apple latitudes where the ribboning geese are headed. These shouts, these sploshes, these hieroglyphic entries into the universal waters are ours – Morgan's and mine – on the Rio Cobre some thousand miles ago. He is with me in the Sligoville summer, running the sweet hours, free of school, of the future, and too young for the past.

We played the fool with the dogs the Rio Cobre, took turns jumping from an overhanging rock into a gorge. The animals splashed around us in the water. One of the dogs, a stray we named Will, elected to make the jump himself. My brother and I turned as one to see Will become a silver jaguar, stiffen in midair, before plunging.

'No Will!' my brother cried.

But Will arrowed straight for the apple of his eye. He applied his teeth to my forehead. Four fine red lines, a perfect 'w' his initial. A red blur came across my sight. I cursed and cuffed at Will, but it was my brother, savvy to his snarling ways, swam up behind and threw his grappling arm around Will's neck, pulled him off of me and swam to the embankment with the damn dog the way you would a drowning man.

My present dog, a black retriever, reads my mind. With a plunge of her own she shatters my reflection. I lift my eyes from the scarlet water. Above the church, over the hill and away to the lines beyond, the trees write their autumnal folio.

Parallax

How well we move along
these lines of latitude
how smoothly voyage out
from home
around, around
are bent unknowing
forward to our beginning.
How each departure clips
into precise return
yet
how suddenly
we are derailed.
And, Mother,
are you there?
If you exist at all –

I don't understand this.

Winnipeg via Rail

Your lines of rail admire this horizon
tent ribs taut sinews holding strain.
Through a moving window
lines of survival and longing
come for you from four directions
point you beyond Europe's old footprint
marked on St Boniface' face.
Beyond America's tiring
tracks the deputies'
forked lines
the executioner's
adjustments
your new breath
arriving in four
directions awakes you.

Pain-ting
for SJM

In this body
grown mortal with the planet
I stand at my easel
painting me
This is how I turned out
All that's here meets the eye
All that can be seen of me
looks back at me in the making

After the treatments
my hair brushed up again
Baby-like at first
Then it bristled, demanding canvas
demanding paint for another self
This is how I turned out
bearing two signatures
The knife's and mine.

KEISHA SILVERA

what lives in the clouds

What lives in the clouds
A fat woman sitting on top of the moon's head
cracked mirror & expanding diaphragms
dogs are biting the feet of the old men singing off key
                      the mediator is fear
                            a shallowed cowardice
                            a pit where words of touch get
                            lost in murky depths
                            a hole of soul & forgotten wrongs
                            my name
My name   embedded in scales
slithering on tongues   swallowed whole
with no way of exit

nine o'clock appointment

I follow with reflexive ease the turmoil of these muddled streets. Lights melt into each other.
Each step avoids puddles of urine or black oil or broken glass. The air is thick and impure and my skin becomes the skin of this city, the coating over which lays all traces of that viscous and ruthless air.
      Lights go on in flashes in the corner of my eyes.
I see them, as more and more people appear peforming intimate gestures and absurd assumptions with their dress. Their heads turn with bird-like accuracy, their movements pixilated. They're watching me because they think I know what the heck I'm doing. (I only know what I must do. I can't see any other way.)

In my "confessional" year (the year that every utterance action breath mattered), everything was possibly TRUTH, and it mattered.
Days and nights were filled with feverish roaming and endless spewing…falling into each other's arms whoever we were at the time...absoloved of any guilt. And the words we spoke and how our bodies kissed each time we touched. Our movements were capped by the convergent sun and moon. It was romance even as we lived it.
And you were so earnest that the trouble that could be drawn from our lives drifted into non-legacy. "Just do it," you said, smiling as always.
And I did.
And was pleased.

The day breaks into full light. Distortions disappear and all of the colours can now be seen. I walk down the street among the voice, the park, the walk, the block that was so…
you.

He rises with the sun every morning out of habit.
He could have been my first thought of restless limbs
and teeth with holes in them.
He could have been desire – glances in between words
and smiles not quite intended.

I wanted to take part in his youth.   I wanted to give
him my kiss.
He was hued like a rainbow.
Each colour sifted out of him like incensed smoke.
He was well aware that I wanted to stroke each and
every strand of his hair
wrap myself backwards around him
my hands clasped through his toes.
I could only stand aloft and watch the contortions of my
body, as it went mad before him a St. Vitus dance.

Now I can but chase the backs of people I see on the
street.
Now I can but chase after people I know are not him.

Of course one foot is in front of me, the other, naturally,
behind.
I could do this forever.
Weighing this and that.
Go this way.
And I will be left searching every area of my body for
just the hint of your presence. I will find a shard of glass,
the same one that performed as a prism reflecting your
colours – the same one that seared off my edges, leaving
me raw, limping and pallid.
Go this way.
And all sources cease to be the quotient equaling life.
This way and like puckered buds we will push our way
out of each other. The one sanguine red and fecund with

all that is potential and the other collapsed
>   destroyed
>   deflated.
I want you to return to me all at once, as it was my love when you were the insinuation and I was the magician.

& then there's the other side of the street

1
broken glass
ttc transfers that are almost $
breeze from a shutting door
Leering loiterers
Latenight launderers
& me not so lonely wanderer

2
When I walk these 4 a.m. streets they are mine
& we
howling but still the moon was not in sight
barking dogs
snorting pigs
kitty cats meow
we mooed like cows
we were drunk with the invisible moon
we left our names in stone
that night the sky sacrificed the moon
to our senseless delight

Lipstick

Lipstick   moist over red
                 the come-fuck-me kind, sun down,
                 soon to be run down smeared onto
                 another, always kissing the wrong
                 person goodnight.
The air is heavy smoke that huffs through the
spotlight. She watches the light crescent his face in
orange as he turns away. First light: the side of his
cheekbones, then the line of his nose, until the face
is full. Full of love, Full of darkness,
   Full of shit, Full of flow &
   always full of you.

American Gothic

They are bound
In their lifestyle
They are bound skintight
Silence is their only option
         windows closed
         curtains closed
mouths closed
fists closed   sealed and dripping at the edges
             with fury or sorrow or some human
emotion
They think they are scared   (if only it mattered)
They think they are True   (if only it mattered)

oranges

oranges
they always make my hands smell
sometimes white under the nails
the white of the rind is caught in them
but your tongue can't reach that far between
fingernail & tip
sweetness buried
fossilized
holes in hard white stone
only teeth remain in once red & fleshy
fleshiness bursting in my mouth
running down along my insides
outside my face that you say is read so
easily
Don't give me that look you said
well it's the only one I have for you
I guess that was the problem all along
we go to a fruit market
and buy one of each colour the orange   the
apple the banana
the pear
and rub each one against our skin
cratered   & you actually like it   that way?!

JANET SOMERVILLE
Calling Card

This morning my brother
came back as a cormorant

left his calling card

an onyx feather
          on the tip
                    of the bow
                              of his boat

a quill I've carved
and dipped into jet ink
to scratch this poem

Italian Touring Tips

In Firenze
the city of lilies

the Gideons have
not left a Bible

instead I find a guide
of local phrases

the two I pledge to practise
sound like antipasto appetizers:

vattene al diavolo
ti hoto aspetta tuta la mia vita

On These Shores

In the late afternoon
the lozenge sun
has moved behind my back
    and I lounge
    in the shade
    of the long-needled pine
out here on pink grey rock
    as the dogs snap at horseflies
    or chase chipmunks (their tails flagpoles
    daring to be captured)
boaters churn indigo water black mother of pearl
trailing squealing children across their rolling wake
    hydraulic pumps thump down shore
    worrying away their business
of recovering a sunken boathouse
its waterlogged boards too tired
to resist gravity's tug
    and a cormorant
        riding currents of cool air
            loops and swirls above the peeling birch

Rowing the Inner Harbour at 6 a.m.

the lake is millpond still
                as the rising sun bruises
                          the north shore mauve
        where scullers stretch
                and drive their piston legs
                        into each finished stroke
and dipping pools ripple echoes
        across the harbour
                sliding precision patterns
as blades slice and catch waves
        to the rhythms of the azure moon

Chez Pierre
for Barry Callaghan

On the outskirts of Albany
on a warm-hearted night in May

we gathered at Chez Pierre
Piaf crooning *"La Vie en Rose"*

and found our fate-flung fête
bursting into song.

Back at the Faun's cottage
nightcapped and cozy

we drifted in the arms of Morpheus
to the rhythm of Hogg's fingers

sliding Beethoven then the Blues
across the ivory and ebony

At the Pietà
Grief turns you to stone. – A.S. Byatt

In San Pietro
in the *Jubilate*
Anno

You never expected
to stand here
in sisterhood with Mary
as she cradles her crucified son
draped in death across her lap

His weight
stone cold
her burden
as the thumb
of his right
hand catches
in the marble folds
of her robe

Michelangelo's marble
is another stone

Precambrian shield
cracked wide
your own
son's skull
not so many
years ago

How could
either man
so young
have known
such agony?

MARY LOU SOUTAR-HYNES

after
shocks

1

     and memory
arrive without warning keep you off
   balance breaking away
 from cover
sleeping out-of-doors away
  from walls from any floor
   above ground

     always on
edge awareness heightened for
   each slight reverberation
the tremors' low intensifying
   rumble

2

    in closed cupboards
   tea cups rattle
a wine glass slides across the surface of
  the bar and crystals chime —
   chandeliers of
  moving light

     where after-shocks are
    heavy cracks appear
dormant recollections surface in rubble
   structures fall in step
    with earth's slow-
   motion tango

beyond the edge

free dive   beyond the edge
light   on weighted rope
just you   the sea and dark
breath   liquid

light   on weighted rope
cold   comes in waves
breath   liquid —
cellular memories one with the sea

cold   comes in waves
hear the crackle   of live coral
cellular memories one with the sea
as the throat sighs open

hear the crackle   of live coral
just you   the sea and dark —
as the throat sighs open
free dive   beyond the edge

tufetto sands

i rushed to Rome
thinking you were dying
sat with you
that sunday   on the hospital balcony
            you   (inhaling a
        forbidden cigarette)
reciting the haiku   written for your son
some days before

no surprise
to find you   closing
death's door firmly   one more time —

returning to these
volcanic hills
tufetto sands from springs and streams
where the earth   breathes   warm and silent

we laugh
late into evening
recalling island-memories —
eccentric casts   worthy   of a playwright's pen

each of us with
aneurysms
marking time —

clusters of oak   face into wind
          plumbago's
sturdy shrub blossoms
blue   Cerulean

sun   fades across tufetto valleys
while mimosa's   green plumes
fan   your sky

harbour front lounge:
casino halifax

1

                decaying hulls
groan   moss-green   against the docks
      the swell and sting of salt
crusting water lines —

      two rusting ships   at
anchor   myths corroding   scored
      by tides

          no view
    of harbour   or of sea
        from this *harbour front*
lounge   as players gamble   their own stories
on silent velvet   blues —
      surfaces   beguiling   as the sea

2

      bets placed
they coil around the tables —
     keep the lay   tight
faking   to the slot machines   the music's
    pulse
         the sea's
              raw canvas

      discerning a subtler
corrosion   in the blackjack callers'
pitch of voice   its
     loose resilience —
         the breaking strain   of rope

transit/ sighting

                          she prays the rosary
                 from *king*   to *finch*
          fingering beads —
 stops   full of grace
decades   measuring
                    distance —
          joyful mysteries perhaps   or sorrow
      tightly wedged   in winter's thick
                  indifference
    compelled to closeness   a door's random offerings

      bodies press   along platform walls   brace
              against wind-shear
                  angles   of trains —

                                                  evoking
                                              rites
                                      their swift
                                  illumination

JENNIFER WALCOTT
San Woman

Small caravans of sweat
traverse the hairpin turns
and aging coruscations
of her patient face.
The flattened forehead leaks
onto the reddened hillock cheeks.
A nod, and lizard-quick her lids
slip, closing secret caverns
from the sun.

Her laughter is lute, tambourine,
drum, rain on dry grass
and wind-whipped desert sand.
She knows life through each pore
of her sun-toughened skin.

This skin is wise, contains
whole narratives for curious, courteous eyes.

Bathurst and Queen

down among the refuse mounds
and gopher holes
by Pizza Pizza
at Bathurst and Queen

loki circles the molehills
and garbage bags
hungrily hunting
hidden butts

way over yonder
on the other side of the prairie wide
street, a blind
of blankets hides
the drunken ducks
who've taken cover
to watch and wait

anancy spins his yarns
round foxy ladies and fly-
by night teens
hoping for a lil' somethin'
not the smirk or spit
he dances over

and coyote,
snuffling round
his sleeping mate
cocks his head and howls
at the moon lighting up this night
alive with shape-shifters, tricksters, fools.

Scars

me, I have
nothing to medicate
her pain.
I just want
to kiss the wrist
on which she has
carved FUCK LIFE
harsh words,
all angles

all I can
give are words
and so I pour
them on her
like a balm
wishing I were
a healer woman
with magic oils

oil of soothe-your-spirit
oil of love-yourself
oil of you-can-cope

I pour
words on her
and hope.

Cerasee

Cerasee flew out one night, swallowed the moon,
whole, and found she had a new career-
purgation via truth-telling, her version, as in:

men iron out women and bind their tongues;
children wring their mother's hearts
daughters especially

nothing dies – just gets stuffed into closets
in your mind; joy is fleeting,
but peace is possible for hours at a time

beware of dark days, they turn you inside out
and never cross bridges alone,
they conjure dreams of flight

but cool coconut water, sunsets
and wet mountain sides wash
off your heart, shower you with light.

Cartoon

Like the suicide bomber's,
Your self sacrifice
I fail to understand.

You struggle to take shape,
Balance dark and light
Find the focal point.

Pulled to negative space
You rail against the frame
Smudge defining lines.

There's no nirvana, love.
Seek repose right here;
Unstrap your bombs and live.

Mapping

I want to make a map of you
trace your contours
pace mountains and valleys
scour your rough bushes, mark out
the plains.
I could make an archeological dig
into your oesophagus
through your heart
right to the very core of you.

I will navigate the rivers of your blood,
scope your thoughts,
scrape out your bowels.

I'll read my maps
use these surveyor's tools
take up pick
axe and chisel to scale
the pinnacle of you.

I'll plant my flag,
turn hermit
and meditate on the
meaning of mapping you.

Split Infinitive

I write of
two countries

one where warm water
runs between my words
rinsing verbs
drowning subjects

And the other

where cold snow
parses my sentences
dangling participles
blanketing objects

And I dream
between worlds.

CONTRIBUTORS

CELIA FERRIER attended undergraduate and graduate school at the University of Toronto, the Arvon Foundation Writers' Workshop at Moniack Mhor, Invernesshire, and the Humber School for Writers. With Yanna McIntosh she wrote *Trace*, a one-woman show produced at Toronto's Fringe Theatre Festival in 1997.

NAN PEACOCKE, a citizen of Canada and St Vincent and the Grenadines, was born in Guyana, and grew up in Trinidad, Venezuela and Jamaica. Based in rural Ontario, she moves between Toronto, St Vincent and Barbados. She is a recipient of a Commonwealth Broadcasting Award 2000 and co-winner of the 2003 Timothy Findley Prize for short fiction.

KEISHA SILVERA (October 18, 1976 – July 8, 2001) is the daughter of Toronto writer, Makeda Silvera. She was born in Toronto into a family of storytellers and is of Jamaican heritage. A gifted poet, most of her work was written between the ages of twenty and twenty-four.

JANET SOMERVILLE is grateful for poet Olive Senior's guidance at the Humber School for Writers Summer Workshop. She workshopped memoir excerpts under Catherine Gildiner's direction at the Banff Centre's Fall 2005 Writing with Style programme. She lives in Toronto where she competes on a Masters Women's rowing crew.

MARY LOU SOUTAR-HYNES, a Jamaican-Canadian, poet/educator and former nun, lives and works in Toronto. *The fires of naming*, her first poetry collection, was published in Toronto by Seraphim Editions in 2001. A member of the League of Canadian Poets, The Writers' Union of Canada, and the Association of Caribbean Women Writers and Scholars, her work has appeared in a variety of journals. *Travelling light*, her second poetry collection, is forthcoming from Seraphim Editions in 2006.

JENNIFER WALCOTT, born and raised in Jamaica, adopted Canada where she has lived for many years. Work in community development, radio, organizational change and secondary education defined much of her life. Now, well into her middle years, she combines teaching English with writing and handicrafts to achieve balance and comfort.

PAMELA MORDECAI has written about Caribbean literature and compiled textbooks and anthologies, mostly of the writing of Caribbean women. She has written plays, short stories, five children's books, three collections of poetry and (with her husband, Martin) a reference work on Jamaica. Sandberry Press published her fourth collection of poetry, *The True Blue of Islands*, in 2005.

EDITOR'S NOTE

In 1980 Heinemann (Caribbean) published a collection of poetry edited by Mervyn Morris and myself called *Jamaica Woman*. It was the first anthology that I worked on, and, to the best of my knowledge, the first collection of poetry by women from the region. It started out to be an anthology of poetry by women from the entire English-speaking Caribbean, but that proved difficult. The countries were far apart, there was no web, no internet, no e-mail, no funding to enable the necessary research, nor to cover travel expenses.

None of the poets in *Jamaica Woman* had at that time published a book of their own – indeed, that was one criterion for inclusion. Many of them would go on to publish not one but several books of poetry. The year, 1980, would become a watershed for the publishing of writing by Caribbean women and the *Jamaica Woman* anthology would be sufficiently in demand for Heinemann (UK) to republish it in 1985.

As for tackling the regional poetry project, that waited until 1992 when, along with my sister, Betty Wilson of the Department of French, University of the West Indies, I edited a special issue of Fairleigh Dickenson University's *The Literary Review*, devoted to the poetry of women from the anglophone, francophone, hispanophone and Dutch Caribbean, with poems in the original languages as well as in translation.

Prior to this, Betty and I had edited the prize-winning anthology of prose fiction by Caribbean women, *Her True-True Name* (1989), and Sister Vision Press had published *Creation Fire* (1990), also an anthology of poetry by Caribbean women presenting poems in their original languages as well as in translation.

The writing of Caribbean women was finally receiving the attention it so richly deserved.

So, why *this* anthology?

Put simply, because it's still not easy for new writers to get published, even in Canada where small presses abound. It is especially hard for *poets* to get published, and moreso for Caribbean heritage poets, many of whom elect to write in the vernacular Englishes of the Caribbean, a choice which can be perceived as limiting the potential audience.

While journals and magazines exist as outlets for two or three poems by a particular poet, an anthology such as this can function like a collection of chapbooks: there can be enough of each poet's work for the reader, in the metaphor of our title, to savour the signature, to contemplate the poet's calling card.

We hope to publish other such collections.

It is true that 'Caribbean/Canadian' in the book's sub-title means both 'Canadian poets of Caribbean heritage' and 'Caribbean as well as Canadian poets'. But the challenge to categorization is deliberate: six women, five of them teachers, the youngest in her early twenties, the oldest in her mid-sixties. Four originally from other countries. Four of Caribbean heritage. Three of African-Caribbean heritage. Three born in the Caribbean. Two gay women. Two mothers. One former nun.

Is their poetry similar in any way?

To answer that, you, gentle reader, must consult the poems. I hope you have as much pleasure in doing so as I had selecting and putting them together.

      Pamela Mordecai
      Toronto, October 2005

ABOUT SANDBERRY PRESS

Sandberry Press publishes Caribbean and Canadian poetry for adults as well as books for children. Founded in 1986 in Jamaica, its main operations moved to Toronto, Canada in 1994.

The emphasis of its modest publication programme is on first collections, and six of these have been published in its Caribbean Poetry Series of nine volumes. *Calling Cards* inaugurates an anthology series that remains true to the first collection focus of the press.

Many people contributed to this first book in the anthology series but it would not have been possible without the expert help of Shivaun Hearne, our publishing consultant, and Robert Harris, who designed our cover. We owe them a big tenk-yuh.